Head of the Class

First Grade

The Complete Collection of First Grade Skills

By Margaret Fetty

Harcourt
Supplemental Publishers
Rigby • Steck-Vaughn

www.steck-vaughn.com

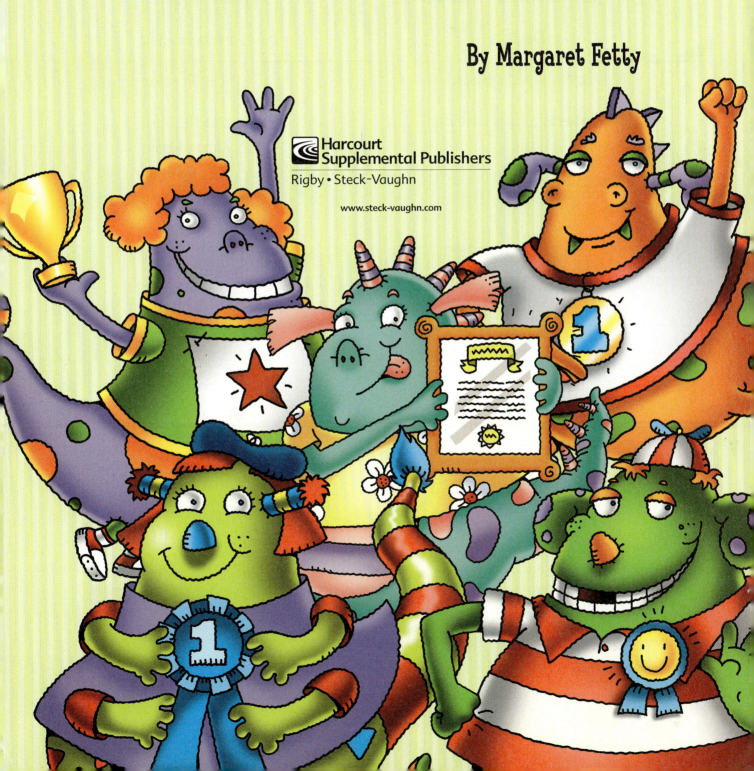

Acknowledgments

Author	Margaret Fetty
Production Coordinator	Perla Arce-Franke
Electronic Production	Gryphon Graphics
Cover Design	Pamela Heaney
Cover Illustration	Ken Bowser
Interior Illustrations	Benone De Lima
	Aaron Romo
	Ken Bowser
	David Chapman

ISBN 0-7398-8361-5

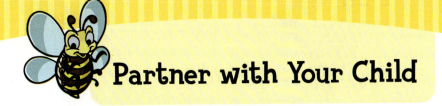

Partner with Your Child

Head of the Class provides enjoyable practice in grade-level skills for your child. It covers the same subjects that are taught in the classroom. You can feel confident using *Head of the Class* because each activity targets a benchmark learning standard required in many states. Moreover, the colorful pages will motivate your child to continue learning long after the school bell rings.

The activities in *Head of the Class* are color-coded by skill and can be used in any order. Use the Skills Checklist on pages 6 and 7 to help you keep track of your child's accomplishments.

Other incentives are included in this book. Each of the eight skill awards on page 127 can be proudly displayed on the refrigerator after your child has completed a group of skills. After receiving all eight awards, your child can turn them over to put together a puzzle. After the book is complete, you can award your child the certificate of completion on page 129. On the back, there is a place for your child to draw a picture showing his or her proudest accomplishment.

When your child is working through the book, encourage him or her to share the learning with you. You will be amazed at how quickly your child does go to the head of the class!

Each activity targets a benchmark learning standard.

How to Help Your Child Learn

- Observe and listen to find out what your child already knows, what is confusing, and what he or she wants to learn.

- Allow your child the time to practice and the freedom to make mistakes.

- Follow these four steps of teaching and learning:

  Step 1 Show your child how.
  Say, *I'll do; you watch.*

  Step 2 Let your child help.
  Say, *I'll do; you help.*

  Step 3 Let your child practice.
  Say, *You do; I'll help.*

  Step 4 Let your child show what he or she has learned.
  Say, *You do; I'll watch.*

Contents

4

First Grade Skills Checklist

Math Skills

Skill	Page	✓	Date
Calendar	93	☐	
Calendar	115	☐	
Classify	58	☐	
Classify	90	☐	
Graph	47	☐	
Graph	103	☐	
Patterns	12	☐	
Patterns	51	☐	
Patterns	99	☐	
Sequence	39	☐	
Sequence	116	☐	

Money

Skill	Page	✓	Date
Money	29	☐	
Money	59	☐	
Money	78	☐	
Money	86	☐	
Money	105	☐	
Money	113	☐	
Money	120	☐	

Computation

Skill	Page	✓	Date
Add Two-Digit Numbers	97	☐	
Add Two-Digit Numbers	118	☐	
Addition Facts to 5	40	☐	
Addition Facts to 8	44	☐	
Addition Facts to 10	49	☐	
Addition Facts to 14	74	☐	
Addition Facts to 18	77	☐	
Estimate	109	☐	
Mixed Practice	67	☐	
Mixed Practice	89	☐	
Mixed Practice	121	☐	
Number Sentences	72	☐	
Subtract Two-Digit Numbers	110	☐	
Subtraction Facts from 5	56	☐	
Subtraction Facts from 8	60	☐	
Subtraction Facts from 10	64	☐	
Subtraction Facts from 14	80	☐	
Subtraction Facts from 18	85	☐	
Word Problems	68	☐	
Word Problems	100	☐	

Geometry

Skill	Page	✓	Date
Circles	12	☐	
Diamonds	35	☐	
Rectangles	29	☐	
Shapes	117	☐	
Squares	24	☐	
Triangles	17	☐	

Measurement

Skill	Page	✓	Date
Length	43	☐	
Length	62	☐	
Length	94	☐	
Time	32	☐	
Time	79	☐	
Time	117	☐	
Weight	75	☐	
Weight	111	☐	

Fractions

Skill	Page	✓	Date
Fourths	106	☐	
Fractions	119	☐	
Halves	73	☐	
Thirds	83	☐	

Number Sense

Skill	Page	✓	Date
Compare Numbers	48	☐	
Compare Numbers	91	☐	
Counting to 5	11	☐	
Counting 6 to 10	15	☐	
Numbers to 30	27	☐	
Numbers to 100	36	☐	
Number Words	18	☐	
Skip-Counting	41	☐	
Skip-Counting	70	☐	
Skip-Counting	75	☐	
Tens and Ones	20	☐	
Tens and Ones	23	☐	

First Grade Skills Checklist

Language Arts

Skill	Page	✔ Date
Action Words	51	
Action Words	82	
Action Words	88	
Action Words	95	
Alphabet	99	
Color Words	54	
Compound Words	81	
Days of the Week	43	
Naming Words	45	
Naming Words	55	
Naming Words	72	
Naming Words	98	
Opposites	122	
Root Words	68	
Root Words	116	
Sentence Endings	78	
Sentence Endings	104	
Sentences	41	
Sentences	50	
Sentences	92	
Sentences	102	
Spelling	104	

Phonics

Skill	Page	✔ Date
Blends with *l*	54	
Blends with *l*	77	
Blends with *r*	63	
Blends with *r*	96	
Blends with *s*	48	
Blends with *s*	70	
Consonant Digraphs	67	
Consonant Digraphs	85	
Consonants	37	
Consonants	46	
Consonants	97	
Consonants	121	
Letters Aa, Bb, Cc	10	
Letters Dd, Ee, Ff	13	
Letters Gg, Hh, Ii	16	
Letters Jj, Kk, Ll	19	
Letters Mm, Nn, Oo	22	
Letters Pp, Qq, Rr	25	
Letters Ss, Tt, Uu	28	
Letters Vv, Ww, Xx	31	
Letters Yy, Zz	34	
Long *a*	53	
Long *e*	57	
Long *i*	61	
Long *o*	65	
Long *u*	69	
Long Vowels	76	
Long Vowels	110	
Rhyming Words	17	

Phonics (cont.)

Skill	Page	✔ Date
Rhyming Words	24	
Rhyming Words	52	
Rhyming Words	108	
Short *a*	21	
Short *e*	26	
Short *i*	30	
Short *o*	33	
Short *u*	38	
Short Vowels	42	
Short Vowels	107	
Syllables	63	
Vowel Digraph *ea*	87	
Vowels with *ar*	59	
Vowels with *er, ir, ur*	82	
Vowels with *or*	74	
Words and Pictures	101	

Reading

Skill	Page	✔ Date
Draw Conclusions	39	
Draw Conclusions	109	
Main Idea	87	
Main Idea	18	
Predicting	35	
Predicting	84	
Predicting	100	
Reading Words	27	
Reading Words	66	
Reading Words	96	
Reading Words	112	
Sentences and Pictures	71	
Sentences and Pictures	114	
Story Characters	14	
Story Characters	107	
Story Settings	91	

First Grade Benchmarks

Benchmarks are standards of achievement. The following are first grade benchmarks. Do not expect that all children will have achieved these first grade benchmarks. Benchmarks are used to guide further practice and to measure progress.

Language Arts

- Recognizes beginning consonants
- Recognizes final consonants
- Recognizes long vowels
- Recognizes short vowels
- Knows beginning blends: *sk, sm, sn, sp, st, sw, tw*
- Knows *l* blends: *bl, cl, fl, gl, pl, sl*
- Knows *r* blends: *br, cr, dr, fr, gr, pr, tr*
- Knows digraphs: *ch, sh, th, ng*
- Knows digraphs: *ea, ie, ee*
- Recognizes *r*-controlled vowels
- Uses onset/rhyme patterns correctly
- Recognizes rhyming words
- Can sound out simple words and recognize syllables
- Recognizes high-frequency sight words and spells them correctly
- Recognizes base/root words
- Uses inflectional endings correctly
- Can recognize compound words
- Can identify characters in a story
- Can identify the setting of a story
- Can identify the main idea of a story
- Can identify the conclusion of a story
- Can make predictions about a story or illustration
- Can make illustrations to match sentences/stories
- Can identify nouns and recognize singular vs. plural forms
- Can identify and capitalize proper nouns (names, places, days/months)
- Can identify verbs
- Can identify and write simple sentences
- Uses end punctuation correctly
- Can print legibly
- Knows alphabetical sequence

Math

- Counts and recognizes numbers to 100
- Counts by 2s to 100
- Counts by 5s to 100
- Counts by 10s to 100
- Knows basic addition facts to 18
- Knows basic subtraction facts to 18
- Understands place value in the ones and tens places
- Adds and subtracts 2-digit numbers without regrouping
- Can write number sentences using +, −, and =
- Compares and orders whole numbers using <, >, and =
- Can identify fractions 1/2, 1/3, 1/4, 3/4, put in order, and understand relationship to whole
- Can name basic geometric shapes
- Can sort by one or two attributes
- Can read and create a graph
- Can measure length and weight
- Can measure using inches
- Can tell time on the hour and half-hour
- Recognizes money and can count amounts using penny, nickel, dime, and quarter
- Completes simple patterns
- Can sequence events
- Estimates sums/differences of 1- and 2-digit numerals
- Knows time passage (days, weeks, months, yesterday, next week)
- Can use a calendar
- Uses problem-solving strategies to complete math problems

First Grade Word List

A
after
again
all
am
an
any
are
as
ask

B
baby
back
bag
balloon
bear
behind
bird
black
boat
book
box
boy
brown
bus
but
by

C
came
cold
could
cry

D
dog
dress
duck

E
eat
every

F
far
first
fly
found
four
from

G
girl
give
goat
going
got

H
had
has
her
him
his
hot
how

I
into

J
just

K
know

L
laugh
let
live
lost

M
made
man
must

N
near
nest
new
no

O
of
old
once
our
out
over

P
picture
please
put

R
ran
read

S
saw
school
she
shoe
show
sing
so
soon
stop

T
take
thank
that
them
then
there
they
think
too

U
under

V
very

W
walk
was
went
were
when
who

Y
yellow

Letters Aa, Bb, Cc

Trace and write the letters.

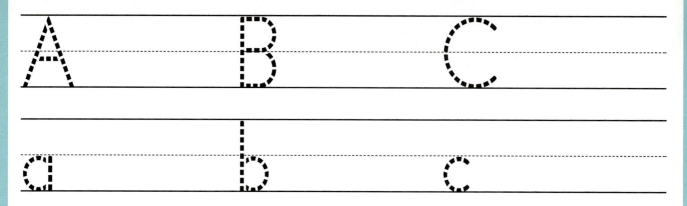

A   B   C

a   b   c

Look at the letters at the beginning of each row. Then read the sentence. Circle the letters that are the same. Finally, draw a line to match the sentence to a picture.

1. **Aa** Ann asked for a hat.

2. **Bb** Ben buys a bat.

3. **Cc** Carla can bake a cake.

Counting to 5

Circle the number to show how many.

1.

2   3   4

2.

3   4   5

3.

1   2   3

4.

1   2   3

5.

3   4   5

Color Patterns

Color the shape to show what comes next.

1.

2.

3.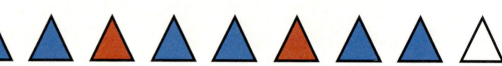

Circles

REMEMBER

circle

Color the circles.

STOP

Letters Dd, Ee, Ff

Trace and write the letters.

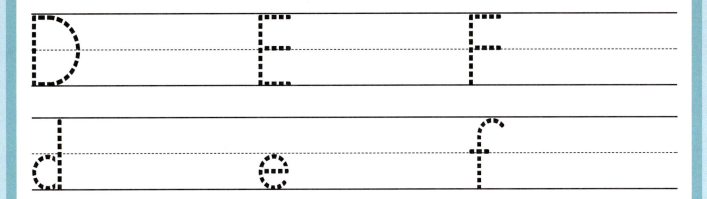

D   E   F

d   e   f

Look at the letters at the beginning of each row. Then read the sentence. Circle the letters that are the same. Finally, draw a line to match the sentence to a picture.

1. **Dd** Did Dan walk the dog?

2. **Ee** Ed saw eggs in a nest.

3. **Ff** Fran has five fish.

Story Characters

Who is the character in each story? Circle the picture.

1. Mrs. Brown walked to the barn. She fed the pigs. She fed the horses. Then Mrs. Brown got the eggs from the hen's nest.

2. Officer Lee put up her hand. The cars stopped. Then she waved to the children. "It is safe to cross the street now," she called. The children thanked Officer Lee.

3. Buzzy Bee was hungry. He went to the kitchen. He got out some honey and peanut butter. He got out the bread, too. Buzzy made a sandwich.

Counting 6 to 10

Circle the number to show how many.

1.

7   8   9

2.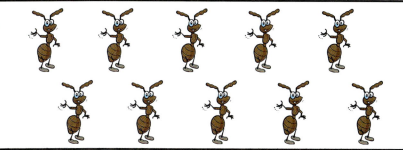

8   9   10

3.

6   7   8

4.

8   9   10

5.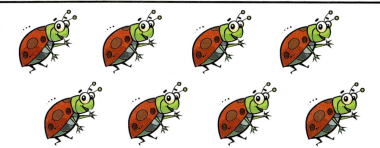

6   7   8

Letters Gg, Hh, Ii

Trace and write the letters.

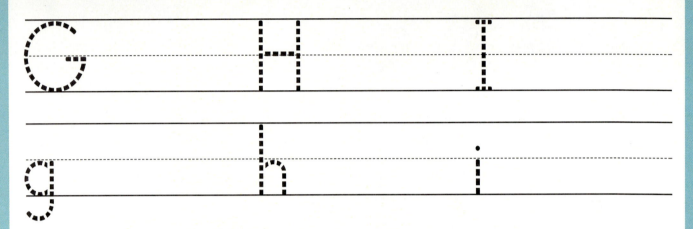

G H I

g h i

Look at the letters at the beginning of each row. Then read the sentence. Circle the letters that are the same. Finally, draw a line to match the sentence to a picture.

1. **Gg** Give Gary the big gift.

2. **Hh** Hal put a hat on his horse.

3. **Ii** Inga wins a pig.

16

Triangles

Color the triangles.

Rhyming Words

Say each picture name. Draw a line to match the pictures whose names rhyme.

1.  2.  3.   4.

Number Words

Read each number word. Draw that many candles on the cake. Then write the number on the line.

 _2_

 ___

 ___

 ___

 ___

 ___

 ___

 ___

 ___

 ___

18

Letters Jj, Kk, Ll

Trace and write the letters.

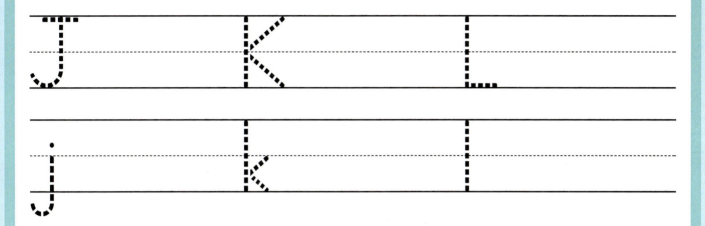

Look at the letters at the beginning of each row. Then read the sentence. Circle the letters that are the same. Finally, draw a line to match the sentence to a picture.

1. **Jj**   Jim gets a jar of jam.

2. **Kk**   Ken takes his kite to the park.

3. **Ll**   Did Liz look for the woolly lamb?

Tens and Ones

Circle ten. Write how many tens and ones.
Then write how many in all.

1. ⭐⭐⭐⭐⭐ ⭐⭐⭐⭐⭐   _1_ ten   _5_ ones

_15_

2. ⭐⭐⭐⭐⭐⭐ ⭐⭐⭐⭐⭐⭐   ___ ten   ___ ones

___

3. ⭐⭐⭐⭐⭐⭐⭐⭐⭐ ⭐⭐⭐⭐⭐⭐⭐⭐   ___ ten   ___ ones

___

4. ⭐⭐⭐⭐⭐⭐⭐ ⭐⭐⭐⭐⭐⭐⭐   ___ ten   ___ ones

___

5. ⭐⭐⭐⭐⭐⭐⭐⭐⭐⭐ ⭐⭐⭐⭐⭐⭐⭐   ___ ten   ___ ones

___

6. ⭐⭐⭐⭐⭐⭐ ⭐⭐⭐⭐⭐⭐   ___ ten   ___ ones

___

Short *a*

Say each picture name. Color the pictures that have the short **a** sound.

Say each picture name. Write **a** if the name has the short **a** sound.

1.

   f___n

2.

   b___t

3.

   j___t

4.

   b___g

5.

   p___n

6.

   m___n

Letters Mm, Nn, Oo

Trace and write the letters.

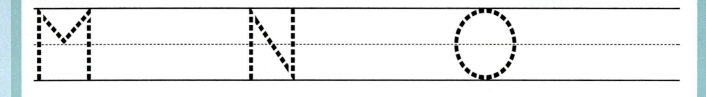

M   N   O

m   n   o

Look at the letters at the beginning of each row. Then read the sentence. Circle the letters that are the same. Finally, draw a line to match the sentence to a picture.

1. **Mm**   Max makes a milk mess.

2. **Nn**   Nan needs a net.

3. **Oo**   Oscar sat on the log.

Tens and Ones

Write how many tens and ones.
Then write how many in all.

1.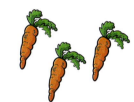

tens	ones
1	3

13

2.

tens	ones

_____

3.

tens	ones

_____

4.

tens	ones

_____

5.

tens	ones

_____

Rhyming Words

Say each picture name. Draw an **X** on the picture whose name does not rhyme.

1.

2.

3.

Squares

Color the squares.

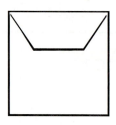

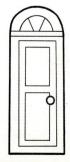

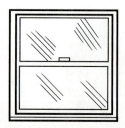

Cracker

Letters Pp, Qq, Rr

Trace and write the letters.

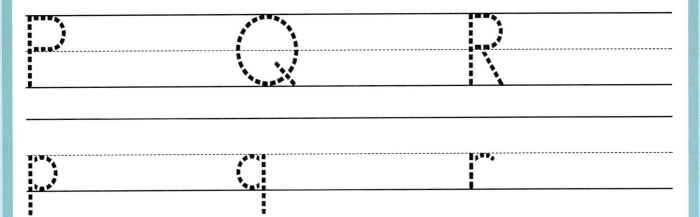

P   Q   R

p   q   r

Look at the letters at the beginning of each row. Then read the sentence. Circle the letters that are the same. Finally, draw a line to match the sentence to a picture.

1. **Pp** Pam pets her pet pig.

2. **Qq** Queen Sue sews the quilt quickly.

3. **Rr** Which race will Rick run in?

Short e

Say each picture name. Color the pictures that have the short **e** sound.

Say each picture name. Write **e** if the name has the short **e** sound.

1.

b____ll

2.

p____n

3.

d____sk

4.

j____t

5.

s____n

6.

l____g

Numbers to 30

Write the missing numbers.

1	2							9	
			14						
									30

Reading Words

Circle the word that names the picture.

1.   can   ran   man

2.   nest   near   neck

3.   dig   dog   dug

Letters Ss, Tt, Uu

Trace and write the letters.

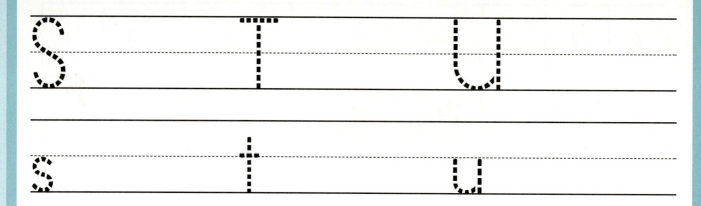

Look at the letters at the beginning of each row. Then read the sentence. Circle the letters that are the same. Finally, draw a line to match the sentence to a picture.

1. **Ss**   Sam sings a song.

2. **Tt**   Tony talks to Tina.

3. **Uu**   Uncle Gus played a drum on the rug.

28

Rectangles

Color the rectangles.

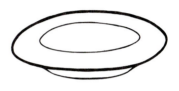

Money

Circle the value of each coin.

1.

1¢   (5¢)   10¢   25¢

2.

(1¢)   5¢   10¢   25¢

3.

1¢   5¢   10¢   (25¢)

4.

1¢   5¢   (10¢)   25¢

Short *i*

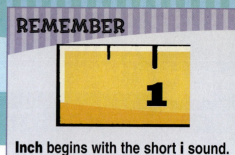
Say each picture name.
Color the pictures that have the short **i** sound.

Say each picture name. Write **i** if the name has the short **i** sound.

1.

w____g

2.

t____p

3.

m____g

4.

b____b

5.

s____x

6.

p____n

Letters Vv, Ww, Xx

Trace and write the letters.

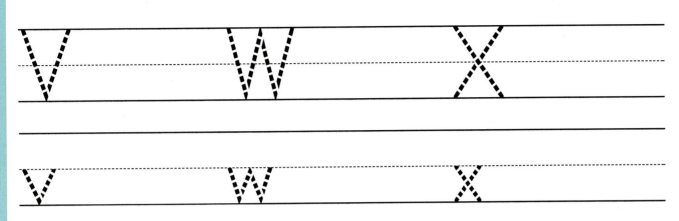

Look at the letters at the beginning of each row. Then read the sentence. Circle the letters that are the same. Finally, draw a line to match the sentence to a picture.

1.  Vera drives the van very slowly.

2.  Wes went for a walk with his dog.

3.  Xavier will mix six cakes.

Time

Write each time two ways.

1.

____3____ o'clock

2.

_____ o'clock

3.

 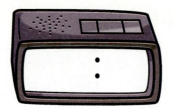

_____ o'clock

4.

 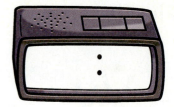

_____ o'clock

5.

 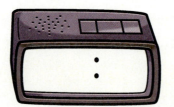

_____ o'clock

6.

 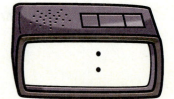

_____ o'clock

Short o

Say each picture name. Color the pictures that have the short **o** sound.

Say each picture name. Write **o** if the name has the short **o** sound.

1.

   m___p

2.

   d___g

3.

   t___p

4.

   f___n

5.

   h___n

6.

   p___t

Letters Yy, Zz

Trace and write the letters.

Y   Z

y   z

Look at the letters at the beginning of each row. Then read the sentence. Circle the letters that are the same. Finally, draw a line to match the sentence to a picture.

1.    Does Yolanda have a yellow yak in her yard?

2. **Zz**   Zack saw a zebra at the zoo.

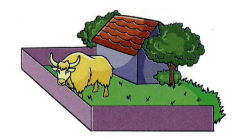

34

Predicting

What will happen next? Darken the circle beside the sentence.

○ The girl will go swimming.

○ The girl will give the dog a bath.

○ The dog will drink water.

Diamonds

Color the diamonds.

REMEMBER

diamond

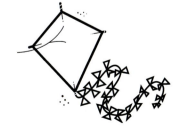

Numbers to 100

Write the missing numbers.

1							8		
								19	
					36				40
				55					
	62								
	82		85						
		93							100

Consonants

Say each picture name. Write the letter for the **beginning** sound.

1.  ____	2.  ____	3.  ____
4.  ____	5.  ____	6.  ____
7.  ____	8.  ____	9.  ____
10.  ____	11.  ____	12.  ____

Short *u*

Say each picture name. Color the pictures that have the short **u** sound.

Say each picture name. Write **u** if the name has the short **u** sound.

1.

s___n

2.

n___ts

3.

b___d

4.

h___g

5.

t___b

6.

w___g

38

Sequence

What is the order? Write 1, 2, and 3.

Draw Conclusions

Read the story. Then darken the circle by the sentence that tells what you know about the boy.

Ken went into the sandwich shop. He asked for the largest sandwich on the menu. Then he ate the sandwich very quickly. Ken felt much better after eating.

O   Ken was late for a ball game.

O   Ken was sick.

O   Ken was very hungry.

Addition Facts to 5

Add.

1.

1 + 1 = _____

2.

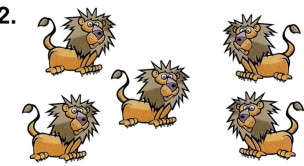

3 + 2 = _____

3.

1 + 2 = _____

4.

2 + 1 = _____

5.

2 + 2 = _____

6.

2 + 3 = _____

Sentences

Read each group of words. Write **yes** if they are a sentence. Write **no** if they are not a sentence.

1. The children went to the park. _____

2. On the slide. _____

3. They laughed loudly. _____

4. Soon they. _____

Skip-Counting

Count by twos. Write how many.

2 _____   4 _____   _____   _____   _____

12 _____   _____   _____   _____   _____

41

Short Vowels

Say each picture name. Circle the letter of the vowel sound you hear.

1.

a e i o u

2.

a e i o u

3.

a e i o u

4.

a e i o u

5.

a e i o u

6.

a e i o u

7.

a e i o u

8.

a e i o u

9.

a e i o u

10.

a e i o u

11.

a e i o u

12.

a e i o u

Length

Color the longer fish  .

Color the shorter fish 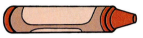 .

1.

_____

2.

Days of the Week

REMEMBER

The names of the days of the week begin with a capital letter.

Write the name of each day correctly.

1. monday _____

2. tuesday _____

3. saturday _____

4. sunday _____

5. friday _____

6. thursday _____

7. wednesday

_____

| ⚽ | ☀️June☀️ | | | | | 🛟 |
Sun.	Mon.	Tues.	Wed.	Thurs.	Fri.	Sat.
		1	2	3	4	5
6	7	8	9	10	11	12
13	14	15	16	17	18	19
20	21	22	23	24	25	26
27	28	29	30			🕶️

Addition Facts to 8

Add. Then color the picture.

4 = 🟥
5 = 🟩
6 = 🟫
7 = 🟨
8 = 🟦

Naming Words

Look at each picture. Does it show a person, a place, or a thing? Write the picture name in the correct column.

children   farm   bike   monkey   cook

bedroom   boy   pie   office   nurse

Person	Place	Thing
_____	_____	_____
_____	_____	_____
_____	_____	_____
_____		

Consonants

Say each picture name. Write the letter for the **ending** sound.

1.
   ____

2.
   ____

3.
   ____

4.
   ____

5.
   ____

6.
   ____

7.
   ____

8.
   ____

9.
   ____

10.
    ____

11.
    ____

12.
    ____

Graph

Complete the picture graph. Draw a balloon to show how many balloons of each color.

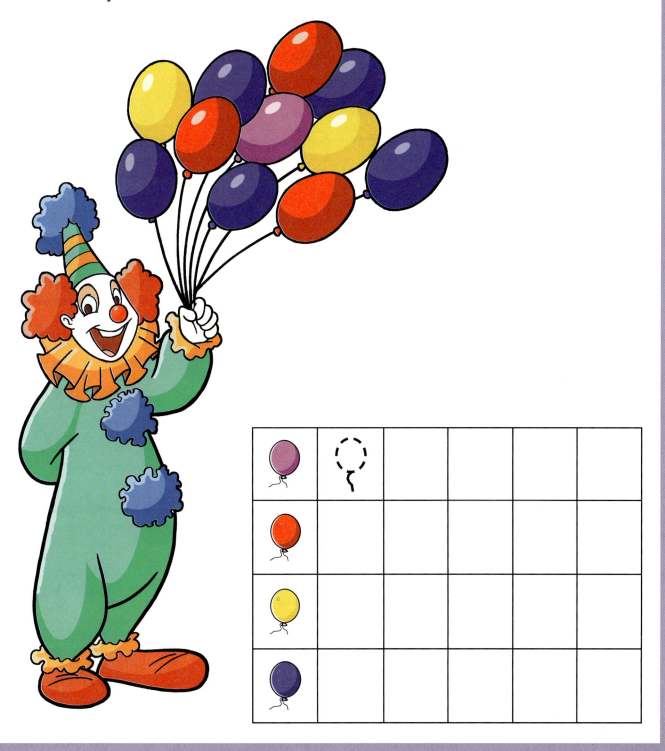

Blends with s

Complete the words. Write **sk**, **sm**, or **st**.

1.

_____amp

2.

_____unk

3.

_____oke

4.

_____ates

5.

_____ile

6.

_____ar

Compare Numbers

Write < or > to make the number sentence true.

1. 22 (<) 35

2. 18 ( ) 12

3. 57 ( ) 53

4. 38 ( ) 83

5. 42 ( ) 68

6. 31 ( ) 41

7. 92 ( ) 90

8. 44 ( ) 84

9. 61 ( ) 59

Addition Facts to 10

Add.

1. $\begin{array}{r} 4 \\ +3 \\ \hline \end{array}$	**2.** $\begin{array}{r} 7 \\ +2 \\ \hline \end{array}$	**3.** $\begin{array}{r} 1 \\ +6 \\ \hline \end{array}$	**4.** $\begin{array}{r} 3 \\ +2 \\ \hline \end{array}$
5. $\begin{array}{r} 2 \\ +5 \\ \hline \end{array}$	**6.** $\begin{array}{r} 8 \\ +2 \\ \hline \end{array}$	**7.** $\begin{array}{r} 3 \\ +7 \\ \hline \end{array}$	**8.** $\begin{array}{r} 4 \\ +4 \\ \hline \end{array}$
9. $\begin{array}{r} 4 \\ +6 \\ \hline \end{array}$	**10.** $\begin{array}{r} 7 \\ +0 \\ \hline \end{array}$	**11.** $\begin{array}{r} 5 \\ +4 \\ \hline \end{array}$	**12.** $\begin{array}{r} 9 \\ +1 \\ \hline \end{array}$
13. $\begin{array}{r} 4 \\ +0 \\ \hline \end{array}$	**14.** $\begin{array}{r} 2 \\ +6 \\ \hline \end{array}$	**15.** $\begin{array}{r} 5 \\ +5 \\ \hline \end{array}$	**16.** $\begin{array}{r} 6 \\ +3 \\ \hline \end{array}$

Sentences

Look at the picture. Then read the groups of words. Complete the groups of words to make sentences that tell about the picture.

1. The school bus _____.

2. The girl _____.

3. A shoe _____.

4. A book _____.

© Steck-Vaughn

Action Words

What is happening in each picture?
Write a word from the box.

1.  _____

2.  _____

3.   _____

4.   _____

5.  _____

6.   _____

eat
walk
play
read
swim
sleep

Size Patterns

Draw the shape that comes next.

1.   _____

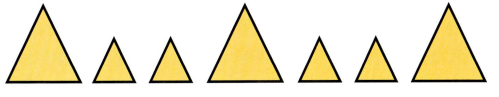

2. _____

3.    _____

Rhyming Words

Read the words. Then write two words that tell about the picture.

1. cat   bat   mat

_____ on a _____

2. hog   log   dog

_____ in a _____

3. net   pet   get

_____ a _____

4. bug   mug   rug

_____ on a _____

Long *a*

Say each picture name. Color the pictures that have the long **a** sound.

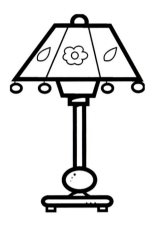  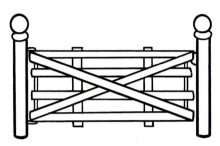

Write a word from the box to complete each sentence.

game   rain   play

1. It began to _____ .

2. The children could not go out

   to _____ .

3. They got out a _____ .

Color Words

Write the words to match the colors.

| red | blue | pink | green | brown | yellow | orange | purple |

1. _____

2. _____

3. _____

4. _____

5.  _____

6. _____

7. _____

8. _____

Blends with l

Complete the words. Write **bl**, **gl**, or **sl**.

1.

_____ue

2.

_____ock

3.

_____eep

4.

_____ue

5.

_____obe

6.

_____ide

54

Long e

Say each picture name. Color the pictures that have the long **e** sound.

Write a word from the box to complete each sentence.

| sea | seal | jeep |

I. Mrs. Ruiz got into her _____.

2. She drove to the _____.

3. Mrs. Ruiz saw a _____.

Classify

Look at the pictures. How would you group them?
Write the group name. Then write the picture name in the
correct column.

apple   yo-yo   wagon   ball

banana   tomato   yolk   kite

_____   _____

_____   _____

_____   _____

_____   _____

Can you think of another way to group the pictures?

Vowels with *ar*

Circle the pictures whose names have the same vowel sound as **car**.

Money

Write how much.

1.  _9_ ¢

2. _5_ ¢

3.  _7_ ¢

4.  _4_ ¢

Subtraction Facts from 8

Subtract.

1. 3
   −1

2. 6
   −6

3. 7
   −6

4. 6
   −2

5. 7
   −3

6. 3
   −0

7. 4
   −1

8. 8
   −3

9. 5
   −4

10. 6
    −3

11. 8
    −4

12. 4
    −3

13. 7
    −5

14. 8
    −6

15. 5
    −2

60

Long *i*

Say each picture name. Color the pictures that have the long **i** sound.

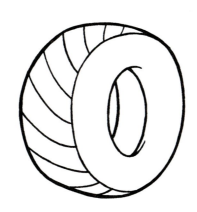

Write a word from the box to complete each sentence.

pie   mile   bike

1. Tim wanted to eat some _____.

2. He got on his _____.

3. He rode to a store that was a _____ away.

Length

How long is each vegetable? Write the number.

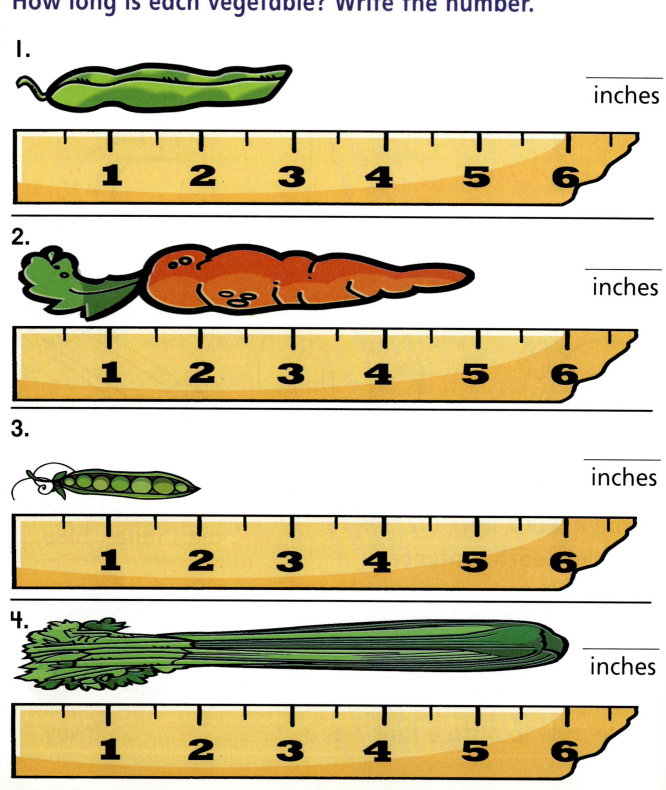

1.

_____ inches

2.

_____ inches

3.

_____ inches

4.

_____ inches

Syllables

Say each picture name. How many syllables do you hear? Write the number.

1. _____

2.  _____

3. _____

4.  _____

5. _____

6. _____

Blends with *r*

Complete the words. Write **br**, **gr**, or **tr**.

1.  _____apes

2.  _____ead

3.  _____een

4.  _____idge

5.  _____ee

6.  _____uck

Subtraction Facts from 10

Subtract. Then color the picture.

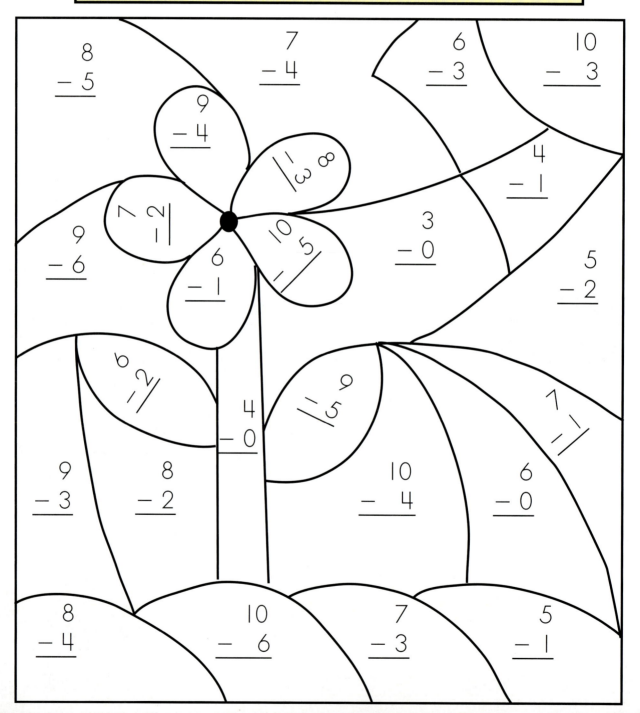

$$\begin{array}{r} 8 \\ -5 \\ \hline \end{array}$$

$$\begin{array}{r} 7 \\ -4 \\ \hline \end{array}$$

$$\begin{array}{r} 6 \\ -3 \\ \hline \end{array}$$

$$\begin{array}{r} 10 \\ -3 \\ \hline \end{array}$$

$$\begin{array}{r} 9 \\ -4 \\ \hline \end{array}$$

$$\begin{array}{r} 8 \\ -3 \\ \hline \end{array}$$

$$\begin{array}{r} 4 \\ -1 \\ \hline \end{array}$$

$$\begin{array}{r} 7 \\ -2 \\ \hline \end{array}$$

$$\begin{array}{r} 9 \\ -6 \\ \hline \end{array}$$

$$\begin{array}{r} 10 \\ -5 \\ \hline \end{array}$$

$$\begin{array}{r} 3 \\ -0 \\ \hline \end{array}$$

$$\begin{array}{r} 5 \\ -2 \\ \hline \end{array}$$

$$\begin{array}{r} 6 \\ -1 \\ \hline \end{array}$$

$$\begin{array}{r} 9 \\ -2 \\ \hline \end{array}$$

$$\begin{array}{r} 9 \\ -5 \\ \hline \end{array}$$

$$\begin{array}{r} 4 \\ -0 \\ \hline \end{array}$$

$$\begin{array}{r} 7 \\ -1 \\ \hline \end{array}$$

$$\begin{array}{r} 9 \\ -3 \\ \hline \end{array}$$

$$\begin{array}{r} 8 \\ -2 \\ \hline \end{array}$$

$$\begin{array}{r} 10 \\ -4 \\ \hline \end{array}$$

$$\begin{array}{r} 6 \\ -0 \\ \hline \end{array}$$

$$\begin{array}{r} 8 \\ -4 \\ \hline \end{array}$$

$$\begin{array}{r} 10 \\ -6 \\ \hline \end{array}$$

$$\begin{array}{r} 7 \\ -3 \\ \hline \end{array}$$

$$\begin{array}{r} 5 \\ -1 \\ \hline \end{array}$$

Long o

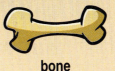

Say each picture name. Color the pictures that have the long **o** sound.

Write a word from the box to complete each sentence.

rose	hose	toad

1. Ann got a water _____.

2. She put water on the _____.

3. The water got a _____ wet.

Reading Words

Write the letter that matches the number.
Then read the words.

a	b	c	d	e	f	g	h	i	j	k	l	m
1	2	3	4	5	6	7	8	9	10	11	12	13

n	o	p	q	r	s	t	u	v	w	x	y	z
14	15	16	17	18	19	20	21	22	23	24	25	26

1. ___ ___ ___
 2 21 19

2. ___ ___ ___
 1 19 11

3. ___ ___ ___ ___
 19 9 14 7

4. ___ ___ ___ ___
 2 15 15 11

5. ___ ___ ___ ___
 18 5 1 4

6. ___ ___ ___ ___ ___
 12 1 21 7 8

7. ___ ___ ___ ___ ___
 20 8 9 14 11

8. ___ ___ ___ ___ ___ ___
 19 3 8 15 15 12

Use two words from above in a sentence.

_____

_____

66

Mixed Practice

Add or subtract.

1. $4 + 3 =$ _____

2. $7 - 5 =$ _____

3. $8 - 2 =$ _____

4. $6 + 3 =$ _____

5. $9 - 9 =$ _____

6. $8 - 1 =$ _____

7. $4 + 6 =$ _____

8. $5 + 5 =$ _____

Consonant Digraphs

Complete the words. Write ch or sh.

1.

_____air

2.

_____eep

3.

_____ick

4.

_____ain

5.

_____oe

6.

_____ell

67

Root Words

Write the root of each word.

1. going _____

2. walks _____

3. played _____

4. stopped _____

5. hugging _____

6. running _____

7. teaches _____

8. painter _____

Word Problems

Write an addition sentence. Then solve.

1. There were 4 ducks swimming. Then 2 more ducks came to swim. How many ducks are swimming now?

___ + ___ = ___ ducks

2. There were 5 ducks looking for bugs. Then 3 more ducks looked for bugs. How many ducks are looking for bugs now?

___ + ___ = ___ ducks

Long *u*

Say each picture name. Color the pictures that have the long **u** sound.

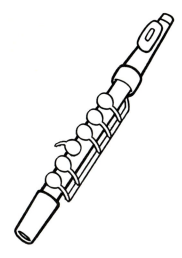

Write a word from the box to complete each sentence.

| tube | tune | huge |

1. Luke has a _____.

2. It is _____.

3. Luke hums a _____.

Skip-Counting

Count by fives. Write how many.

5   10   _____   _____   _____

_____   _____   _____   _____   _____

Blends with *s*

Complete the words. Write sn, sp, or sw.

1.

_____ im

2.

_____ ake

3.

_____ oon

4.

_____ ider

5.

_____ ow

6.

_____ ing

Sentences and Pictures

Read each sentence. Draw a picture to go with it.

1. Fran waters the flowers.

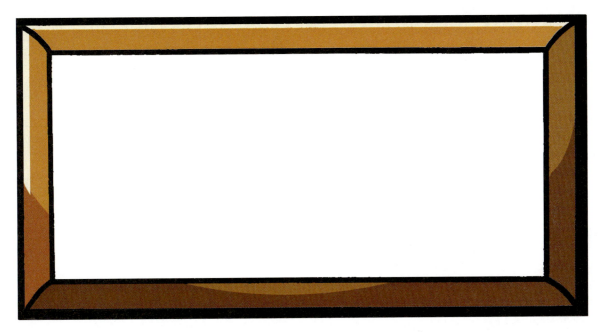

2. Fran's dog plays in the water.

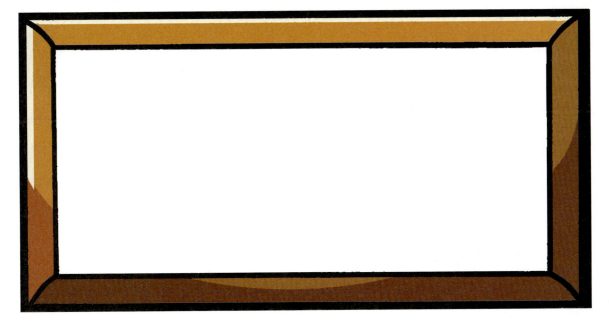

Naming Words

Read each word. Write the name of a special person, place, or thing.

1. girl   _____ Anna _____

2. friend   _____

3. school   _____

4. book   _____

Number Sentences

Write +, –, or = to make each number sentence true.

1. 4 ◯ 2 = 6

2. 8 – 3 ◯ 5

3. 7 ◯ 1 = 8

4. 9 ◯ 5 = 4

5. 5 – 5 ◯ 0

6. 6 ◯ 5 = 1

7. 10 ◯ 7 = 3

8. 4 ◯ 4 = 8

Halves

Circle the shapes that show halves.

1.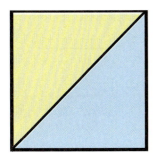

2.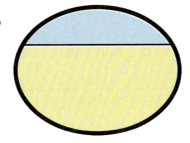

3.

4.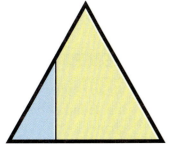

5.

6.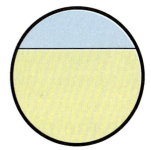

Color $\frac{1}{2}$.

7.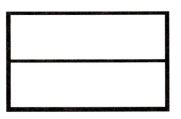

8.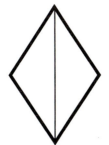

9.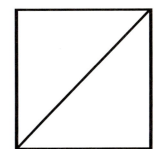

Addition Facts to 14

Add.

1. $5 + 6 =$ _____

2. $7 + 7 =$ _____

3. $9 + 3 =$ _____

4. $8 + 5 =$ _____

5. $\begin{array}{r} 7 \\ +4 \\ \hline \end{array}$

6. $\begin{array}{r} 6 \\ +8 \\ \hline \end{array}$

7. $\begin{array}{r} 9 \\ +4 \\ \hline \end{array}$

8. $\begin{array}{r} 6 \\ +6 \\ \hline \end{array}$

Vowels with *or*

Circle the pictures whose names have the same vowel sound as **corn.**

Weight

About how much does each weigh?
Circle the better estimate.

1.

2 ounces   2 pounds

2.

8 ounces   8 pounds

3.

30 pounds   30 tons

4.

2 pounds   2 tons

Skip-Counting

Count by tens. Write how many.

_10_   _20_   _____   _____   _____

_____   _____   _____   _____   _____

75

Long Vowels

Say each picture name. Circle the letter of the vowel sound you hear.

1.	2.	3.	4.

a e i o u	a e i o u	a e i o u	a e i o u

5.	6.	7.	8.

a e i o u	a e i o u	a e i o u	a e i o u

9.	10.	11.	12.

a e i o u	a e i o u	a e i o u	a e i o u

Blends with *l*

Complete the words. Write **cl**, **fl**, or **pl**.

1.

_____ate

2.

_____own

3.

_____ower

4.

_____ug

5.

_____y

6.

_____ock

Addition Facts to 18

Add.

1.   8
    +7
   ____

2.   9
    +9
   ____

3.   6
    +5
   ____

4.   7
    +6
   ____

5.   8
    +8
   ____

6.   9
    +7
   ____

7.   9
    +8
   ____

8.   6
    +9
   ____

Sentence Endings

Write . or ? or ! to complete each sentence.

1. Jill went fishing _____

2. Wow, look at the big fish she caught _____

3. Do you know what Jill did _____

4. She let the fish go _____

5. Can you believe she let the fish go _____

Money

Write how much.

1.

_____ ¢

2.

_____ ¢

3.

_____ ¢

4.

_____ ¢

Time

Draw hands on each clock to show each time.

1.

2.

3.

4.

5.

6.

Subtraction Facts from 14

Subtract.

1.   11
   − 6

2.   13
   − 5

3.   12
   − 6

4.   12
   − 5

5.   14
   − 9

6.   13
   − 6

7.   11
   − 3

8.   12
   − 3

9.   11
   − 7

10.   10
   − 5

11.   14
   − 8

12.   13
   − 9

13.   14
   − 7

14.   12
   − 4

15.   11
   − 2

Compound Words

Write the words together as a compound word. Then draw a picture of the compound word.

1.   rain + bow

_____

2.   bird + house

_____

3.   lady + bug

_____

4.   foot + ball

_____

Action Words

Circle the word that correctly completes the sentence.

1. Yesterday, Rita and Jen (walk, walked) to the park.

2. They (want, wanted) to swing.

3. They (play, played) on the slide, too.

4. Today, the girls (want, wanted) to bake cookies.

5. They (look, looked) for a good recipe.

Vowels with *er, ir, ur*

Write words from the box to name the pictures.

girl		
fern		
herd		
shirt		
nurse		
church		

1.

_____

2.

_____

3.

_____

4.

_____

5.

_____

6.

_____

Thirds

Circle the shapes that show thirds.

1.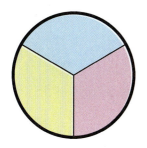

2.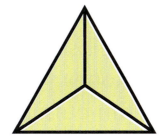

3.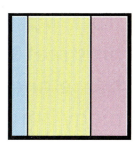

4.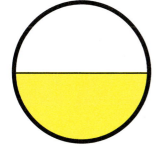

5.

6.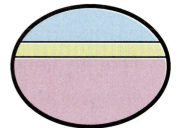

Color $\frac{1}{3}$.

7.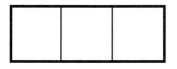

8.

9.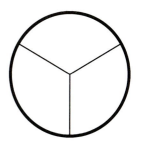

© Steck-Vaughn

Predicting

Read each story. Then circle the picture that tells what will happen next.

1. Sam heard the music. The ice cream truck was coming. It would turn down his street soon. Sam ran inside the house and got some money from his piggy bank. Then he ran outside and waited in front of his house for the truck to stop.

2. Tina gave a big yawn. She was feeling very tired. Tina decided that she would not read tonight. She brushed her teeth and washed her face. Then Tina changed into her pajamas.

3. The bird sat up high in the tree. It looked from side to side. Soon, the bird saw a bug stop on a nearby twig. The bird hopped over to the bug.

Subtraction Facts from 18

Subtract.

1. $15 - 6 =$ _____

2. $17 - 9 =$ _____

3. $16 - 8 =$ _____

4. $18 - 9 =$ _____

5.
$$\begin{array}{r} 17 \\ -\ 8 \\ \hline \end{array}$$

6.
$$\begin{array}{r} 16 \\ -\ 9 \\ \hline \end{array}$$

7.
$$\begin{array}{r} 14 \\ -\ 6 \\ \hline \end{array}$$

8.
$$\begin{array}{r} 15 \\ -\ 7 \\ \hline \end{array}$$

Consonant Digraphs

**Say each picture name. What ending sound do you hear?
Write ck or ng.**

1.

_____

2.

_____

3.

_____

4.

_____

5.

_____

6.

_____

Money

Write how much.

1.

_6_ ¢

2.

_9_ ¢

3.

_11_ ¢

4.

_14_ ¢

5.

_18_ ¢

6.

_22_ ¢

Vowel Digraph *ea*

Write the word that matches each picture.

1.
   _____

2.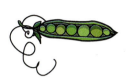
   _____

3.
   _____

4.
   _____

5.
   _____

6.
   _____

bead

pea

spread

thread

leaf

sweater

Main Idea

Read the story. What is this story mostly about? Darken the circle by the sentence.

Sam made a ball out of the snow. Then he rolled it around on the ground. Soon he had a big snowball. Sam made another snowball. But this one was smaller. He put it on the big ball. Then, Sam added two eyes, a nose, and a mouth. Sam thought his snowman looked great!

○ Sam made a snowman.

○ Sam made a snowball.

○ Sam played with his friends.

Action Words

Circle the word that correctly completes the sentence.

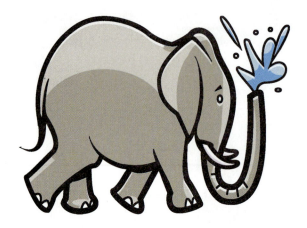

1. Lana and Mary (walk, walks) to the zoo.

2. Lana (want, wants) to see the seals.

3. The seals (swim, swims) quickly through the water.

4. Mary (hope, hopes) to see the lions.

5. She (think, thinks) one lion has cubs.

6. Both girls (enjoy, enjoys) watching the elephants.

7. The elephants (throw, throws) water into the air with their trunks.

Mixed Practice

Add or subtract.

1.
$$\begin{array}{r} 5 \\ +9 \\ \hline \end{array}$$

2.
$$\begin{array}{r} 13 \\ -\ 6 \\ \hline \end{array}$$

3.
$$\begin{array}{r} 11 \\ -\ 8 \\ \hline \end{array}$$

4.
$$\begin{array}{r} 8 \\ +9 \\ \hline \end{array}$$

5.
$$\begin{array}{r} 4 \\ +7 \\ \hline \end{array}$$

6.
$$\begin{array}{r} 9 \\ +9 \\ \hline \end{array}$$

7.
$$\begin{array}{r} 12 \\ -\ 8 \\ \hline \end{array}$$

8.
$$\begin{array}{r} 14 \\ -\ 5 \\ \hline \end{array}$$

9.
$$\begin{array}{r} 5 \\ +5 \\ \hline \end{array}$$

10.
$$\begin{array}{r} 16 \\ -\ 7 \\ \hline \end{array}$$

11.
$$\begin{array}{r} 8 \\ +4 \\ \hline \end{array}$$

12.
$$\begin{array}{r} 18 \\ -\ 9 \\ \hline \end{array}$$

Classify

Draw an X on the picture that does not belong.

1.

2.

3.

  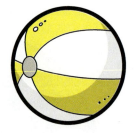 

4.

90

Compare Numbers

Write < or > to make the number sentence true.

1. 43 (<) 47   2. 52 ◯ 25   3. 60 ◯ 59

4. 91 ◯ 89   5. 74 ◯ 72   6. 62 ◯ 26

7. 40 ◯ 50   8. 33 ◯ 43   9. 99 ◯ 89

Story Settings

Write an **X** next to each word that could be a story setting.

1. bridge _____   2. dress _____

3. farm _____   4. school _____

5. boy _____   6. garden _____

7. cake _____   8. train _____

Sentences

Write each sentence correctly.

1. Afrogisgreen.

_____

2. Frogsliketohop.

_____

3. Frogscanswim.

_____

4. Theyeatflies.

_____

Calendar

Use the calendar to answer the questions.

June

Sunday	Monday	Tuesday	Wednesday	Thursday	Friday	Saturday
		1	2	3	4	5
6	7	8	9	10	11	12
13	14	15	16	17	18	19
20	21	22	23	24	25	26
27	28	29	30			

1. What is the name of this month? _____

2. On what day does this month begin? _____

3. How many Saturdays are in this month? _____

4. How many days are in this month? _____

5. On what day does this month end? _____

6. Which day is June 21? _____

Length

Cut out the ruler. Use the ruler
to measure how far each moves.
Then write the number.

> **REMEMBER**
> Line up the 0 on the
> ruler with beginning of
> each path.

1.

_____ inches

2.

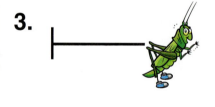

_____ inches

3.

_____ inch

4.

_____ inches

5.

_____ inches

94

Action Words

chop   chopping

Add ing to each word.

1. trip _____

2. begin _____

3. win _____

4. run _____

Write a word from above to complete each sentence.

5. Lee and Tim are _____ a race.

6. The race is _____ now.

7. Tim is _____ over his shoelaces.

8. Lee is _____ the race.

Reading Words

Look at each picture. Circle the word that names the picture.

1.    bag   baby   balloon

2.   goat   going   got

3.    shoe   show   she

Blends with *r*

Complete the words. Write **br**, **dr**, or **pr**.

1.

_____ess

2.

_____ice

3.

_____ick

4.

_____ize

5.

_____ead

6.

_____um

Add Two-Digit Numbers

Add.

1.

tens	ones
1	1
+	3
1	4

2.

tens	ones
2	4
+	2

3.

tens	ones
3	0
+	5

4.

tens	ones
2	7
+	2

5.

tens	ones
4	3
+	5

6.

tens	ones
6	2
+	4

Consonants

Say each picture name. Write the letter for the **beginning** sound.

1.

_____

2.

_____

3.

_____

4.

_____

5.

_____

6.

_____

7.

_____

8.

_____

Naming Words

Read each sentence. Which word or words begin with a capital letter? Write each sentence correctly.

1. Where does jan live?

_____

2. She lives on west road.

_____

3. She lives near mr. carlos.

_____

4. Jan goes to spring school.

_____

Alphabet

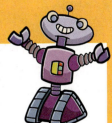

Write the missing letters to show ABC order.

1. c _____ e

2. t _____ v

3. q _____ s

4. m _____ o

5. w _____ y

6. e _____ g

7. i _____ k

8. b _____ d

Patterns

Draw the toy that comes next.

1.

2.

3.

Word Problems

Write a subtraction sentence. Then solve.

1. Clara Clown has 13 balloons. She gives 5 balloons away. How many balloons does Clara have left?

_____ − _____ = _____ balloons

2. The next day, Clara Clown has 16 balloons. She gives 9 balloons away. How many balloons does Clara have left?

_____ − _____ = _____ balloons

Predicting

Read the story. Circle the picture that answers the question.

Juan played a game at the school fair. A big bag was filled with many things. Juan had to put his hand in the bag. He had to guess one of the items in the bag by feeling it. When Juan put his hand in the bag, he felt something long and thin. It was made mostly of wood. But one end felt like hair. What did Juan feel?

Words and Pictures

Say each letter sound as you trace the line. Then say the sounds together. Write the word. Draw a line to match the word to its picture.

1. 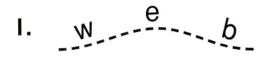 w e b

_____

2. f o x

_____

3. v a n

_____

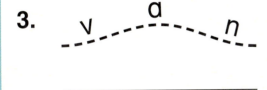

4. c u p

_____

5. p i n

_____

Sentences

Look at the picture. Then read the words in the box. Use words from the box to write at least three sentences about the picture.

vet	sick	look	help	happy

_____

_____

_____

_____

Graph

Look at the graph. Then answer the questions.

The 23 students in Miss Tran's class voted for their favorite pet. The children made a graph to show their findings.

Pets

	1	2	3	4	5	6	7	8	9	10
Dogs	■	■	■	■	■	■	■	■	■	
Cats	■	■	■	■	■					
Birds	■	■	■							
Fish	■	■	■	■						
Turtles	■									

I. How many children voted for cats? _____

2. Which pet did the most children vote for? _____

3. Which pets did the same number of children vote for? _____

4. How many more children voted for dogs than voted for turtles? _____

Sentence Endings

REMEMBER

A period (.) ends a telling sentence.

A question mark (?) ends an asking sentence.

An exclamation point (!) ends a sentence that shows strong feeling.

Write . or ? or ! to complete each sentence.

1. Kim and Lee go for a bike ride _____

2. Look out for that rock, Kim _____

3. Kim fell off her bike _____

4. What can Lee do to help _____

5. Lee finds a neighbor to help _____

Spelling

Look at each group of words. Circle the word that is spelled correctly.

1.		yellow	yello	yeloe
2.		bouk	book	bock
3.		laph	lauf	laugh
4.		ferst	furst	first
5.		picture	pictcher	pikcher

Money

Count on by writing how much.
Then write how much money in all.

1.

__10__ ¢ __11__ ¢ __12__ ¢ __13__ ¢   __13__ ¢

2.

__10__ ¢ __15__ ¢   __15__ ¢

3.

__10__ ¢ __15__ ¢ __16__ ¢ __17__ ¢   __17__ ¢

4.

__10__ ¢ __20__ ¢ __21__ ¢ __22__ ¢ __23__ ¢ __24__ ¢ __24__ ¢

5.

__10__ ¢ __20__ ¢ __30__ ¢ __35__ ¢ __36__ ¢ __37__ ¢ __37__ ¢

Fourths

Circle the shapes that show fourths.

1.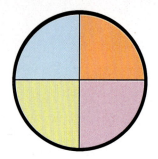

2.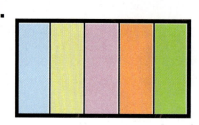

3.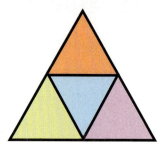

4.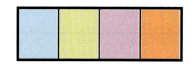

5.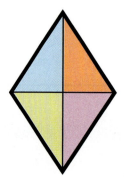

6.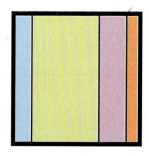

Color $\frac{1}{4}$.

7.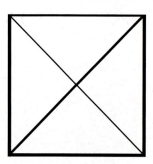

8.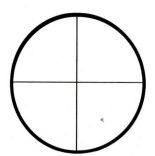

9.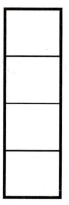

106

© Steck-Vaughn

Short Vowels

Say each picture name. Write **a, e, i, o,** or **u** to tell the short vowel sound you hear.

1.  _____	2. _____	3. _____	4. _____
5. _____	6. _____	7. _____	8.  _____

Story Characters

Read the story. Then read each question. Darken the circle next to the best answer.

Carla was cleaning her room. She found a small ball. She threw the ball into her closet. Then, a small kitten ran out from under the bed. Carla laughed. "Daisy, you are such a funny pet," she said.

1. Who is Carla?

○ a girl

○ a kitten

○ a teacher

2. Who is Daisy?

○ a dog

○ a bird

○ a kitten

Rhyming Words

Write the word that completes each rhyme.

1.

If I were a bug,

I'd dance on a _____.

log   bag   rug

2.

It's fun to run

Out in the _____.

sun   fan   pin

3.

Ella will bake

A chocolate _____.

cake   bike   peek

4.

The little black cat

Fell asleep in a _____.

hit   hot   hat

Estimate

Circle the better estimate.

1.

$$\begin{array}{r} 10 \\ + 10 \\ \hline \end{array}$$

more than 30
less than 30

2.

$$\begin{array}{r} 40 \\ - 20 \\ \hline \end{array}$$

more than 10
less than 10

3.

$$\begin{array}{r} 20 \\ + 20 \\ \hline \end{array}$$

more than 30
less than 30

4.

$$\begin{array}{r} 50 \\ - 40 \\ \hline \end{array}$$

more than 20
less than 20

Draw Conclusions

Read the story. Then darken the circle by the sentence that tells what you know about Gina.

Gina likes to draw elephants. She has a large elephant picture in her bedroom. She always reads books about elephants, too. When Gina went to the zoo, she went to see the elephants first.

○ Gina goes to the zoo often.

○ Gina's favorite animal is the elephant.

○ Gina likes to read.

Long Vowels

Say each picture name. Write **a**, **e**, **i**, **o**, or **u** to tell the long vowel sound you hear.

1.  _____	2.  _____	3. _____	4. 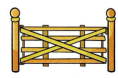 _____
5.  _____	6. _____	7.  _____	8.  _____

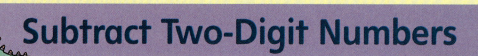

Subtract Two-Digit Numbers

Subtract.

REMEMBER

First subtract the ones.

Then subtract the tens.

1.
tens	ones
1	5
−	2
1	3

2.
tens	ones
1	9
−	8

3.
tens	ones
2	4
−	4

4.
tens	ones
2	8
−	7

5.
tens	ones
3	3
−	1

6.
tens	ones
5	7
−	3

110

Weight

What weighs less than one pound? Color each item.

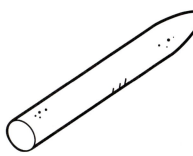

What weighs more than one pound? Color each item.

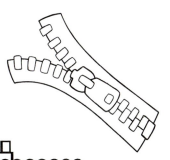

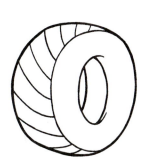

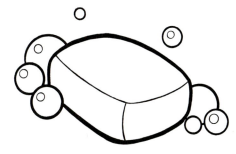

111

Reading Words

Write a word from the box to complete each sentence.

him   bird   bear   duck   walk   behind

1. Carl went for a _____ in the woods.

2. He saw a _____ in a tree.

3. He also saw a _____ swimming on a pond.

4. Carl was surprised to see a big, brown _____

walking in the woods, too.

5. Carl hid _____ a tree.

6. Carl did not want the bear to

see _____ .

Money

Count on by writing how much.
Then write how much money in all.

1.

25 ¢   50 ¢   50 ¢

2.

_____ ¢   _____ ¢   _____ ¢   _____ ¢

3.

_____ ¢   _____ ¢   _____ ¢

4.

_____ ¢   _____ ¢   _____ ¢

5.

_____ ¢   _____ ¢   _____ ¢   _____ ¢   _____ ¢

Sentences and Pictures

Read each sentence. Draw a picture to go with it.

1. Hank blew out the candles on his birthday cake.

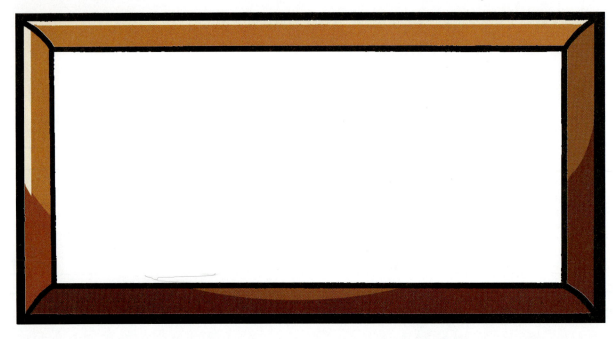

2. Mrs. Smith gave Hank a puppy for his birthday.

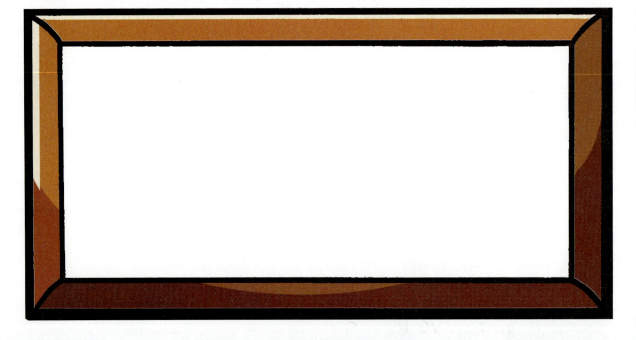

Calendar

Use the calendar to answer the questions.

Sunday	Monday	Tuesday	Wednesday	Thursday	Friday	Saturday
					1	2
3	4	5	6	7	8	9
10	11	12	13	14	15	16
17	18	19	20	21	22	23
24	25	26	27	28	29	30
31						

January

1. Neisha's birthday is January 6. What day is Neisha's birthday? _____

2. What is the day before Neisha's birthday? _____

3. What is the date one week after Neisha's birthday? _____

4. Neisha will have her birthday party on January 9. What day will Neisha have her party? _____

5. Neisha takes piano lessons each Friday. How many lessons will Neisha have in January? _____

Root Words

Write the root of each word.

1. ducks _____

2. pans _____

3. boxes _____

4. boats _____

5. dresses _____

6. foxes _____

7. bikes _____

8. glasses _____

Sequence

What is the order? Write 1, 2, and 3.

1.

☐   ☐   ☐

2.

☐   ☐   ☐

116

© Steck-Vaughn

Shapes

How many of each shape do you count? Write the number. Then color the picture.

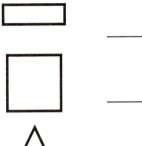

_____

_____

_____

_____

Time

Write each time.

1.  _____ : _____

2.  _____ : _____

3.  _____ : _____

4.  _____ : _____

Add Two-Digit Numbers

Add.

1.

tens	ones
1	2
+1	3
2	5

2.

tens	ones
1	6
+1	1

3.

tens	ones
1	8
+1	0

4.

tens	ones
2	5
+1	4

5.

tens	ones
3	0
+2	3

6.

tens	ones
4	7
+3	1

Main Idea

Read the story. Darken the circle by the best title.

Raccoon was very hungry. What could he find to eat? He took a big breath. He smelled something sweet. Raccoon walked toward the smell. It came from a tree. He climbed up, up, up. Raccoon found a hole and put his hand inside.

"Honey!" said Raccoon. "What a nice snack!"

○ Raccoon Looks for a Friend
○ A Hungry Raccoon
○ How Bees Make Honey

118

Fractions

What part is shaded? Circle the fraction.

1.

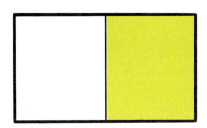

$\frac{1}{2}$ $\frac{1}{4}$

2.

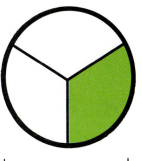

$\frac{1}{3}$ $\frac{1}{5}$

3.

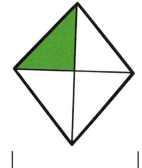

$\frac{1}{2}$ $\frac{1}{4}$

4.

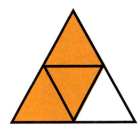

$\frac{2}{4}$ $\frac{3}{4}$

5.

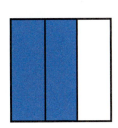

$\frac{1}{3}$ $\frac{2}{3}$

6.

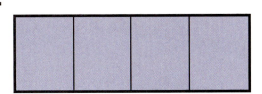

$\frac{4}{4}$ $\frac{1}{4}$

Money

Draw lines to match the food with its amount.

1.  40¢

2.  95¢

3.  32¢

4.  77¢

5.  58¢

120

Mixed Practice

Add or subtract.

1. $\begin{array}{r} 11 \\ +\ 6 \\ \hline \end{array}$

2. $\begin{array}{r} 19 \\ -\ 3 \\ \hline \end{array}$

3. $\begin{array}{r} 25 \\ +\ 4 \\ \hline \end{array}$

4. $\begin{array}{r} 36 \\ -\ 2 \\ \hline \end{array}$

5. $\begin{array}{r} 45 \\ -25 \\ \hline \end{array}$

6. $\begin{array}{r} 53 \\ +46 \\ \hline \end{array}$

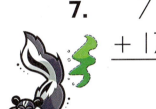

7. $\begin{array}{r} 71 \\ +17 \\ \hline \end{array}$

8. $\begin{array}{r} 93 \\ -51 \\ \hline \end{array}$

Consonants

Say each picture name. Write the letter for the ending sound.

1.
    _____

2.
    _____

3.
    _____

4.
    _____

5.
    _____

6.
    _____

7.
    _____

8.
    _____

Opposites

Read each clue. Write a word from the box that means the opposite. Then write the word in the puzzle.

| hot | girl | near | under | laugh | found |

Across

4. far _____

5. cry _____

Down

1. boy _____

2. over _____

3. lost _____

6. cold _____

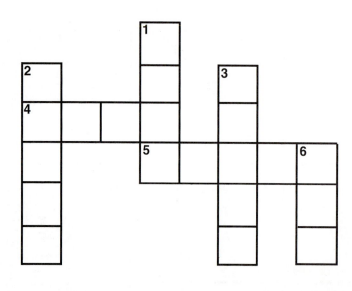

Going high or going low—
it's getting late.
Come on! Let's go!

Let's Go!

My bags are packed.
Today is the day.
I'm ready to leave and go far away.

It might be fun to take a trip
to the moon in a rocket ship.

How would you like to ride up high
in a balloon that floats
through the sky?

I'll take a bus, a car, or a train.
I'll even ride in an airplane.

There is so much to do and see.
Why don't you come along with me!

3

A boat ride might be lots of fun.
We'll sail all day out in the sun.

4

I Know the long and short vowels!

I Know the consonant blends!

I Know about naming words!

I Know about action words!

I Know the math facts!

I can count to 100!

I can count money!

I can tell time to the hour and half hour!

128

I DID IT!

_____

Name

I am at the
Head of the Class!

What are you proud of? Draw a picture.
Then complete the sentence.

I am proud because I

_____

_____

_____ .

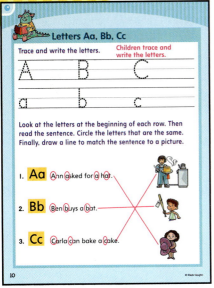

Page 10

Page 11

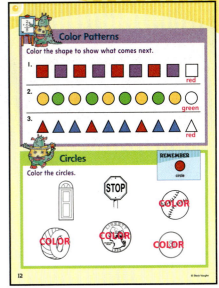

Page 12

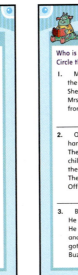

Page 13

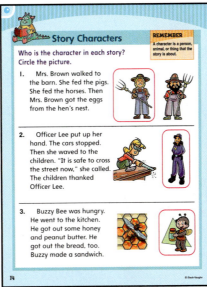

Page 14

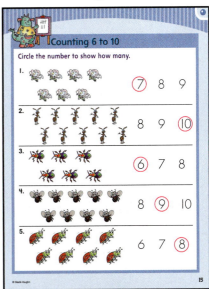

Page 15

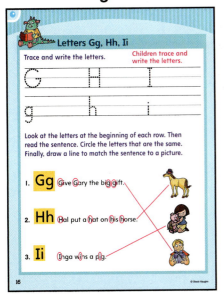

Page 16

Page 17

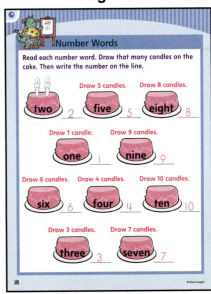

Page 18

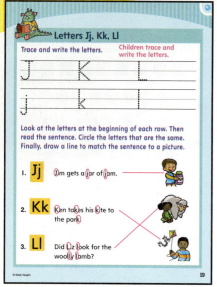

Page 19

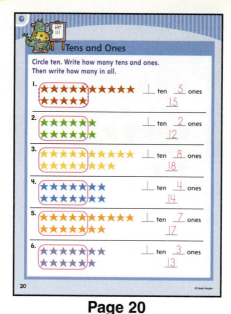

Page 20

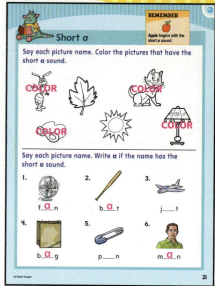

Page 21

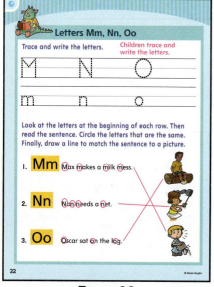

Page 22

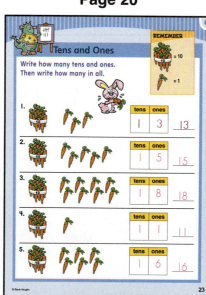

Page 23

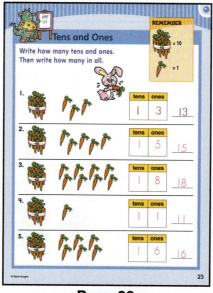

Page 24

Page 25

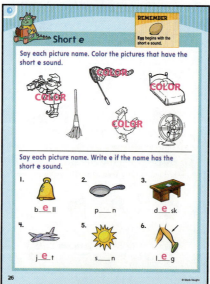

Page 26

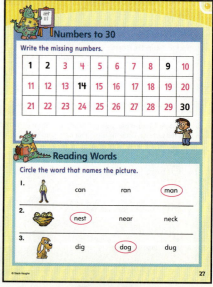

Page 27

132

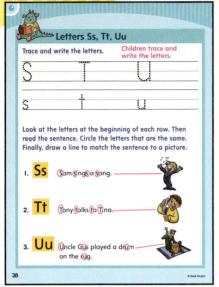

Letters Ss, Tt, Uu

Trace and write the letters.

Children trace and write the letters.

S T U

s t u

Look at the letters at the beginning of each row. Then read the sentence. Circle the letters that are the same. Finally, draw a line to match the sentence to a picture.

1. Ss — Sam sings a song.

2. Tt — Tony talks to Tina.

3. Uu — Uncle Gus played a drum on the rug.

Page 28

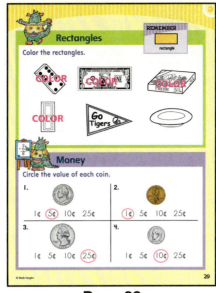

Rectangles

REMEMBER — rectangle

Color the rectangles.

COLOR   COLOR   COLOR   COLOR

Money

Circle the value of each coin.

1. 1¢ 5¢ 10¢ 25¢   2. 1¢ 5¢ 10¢ 25¢
3. 1¢ 5¢ 10¢ 25¢   4. 1¢ 5¢ 10¢ 25¢

Page 29

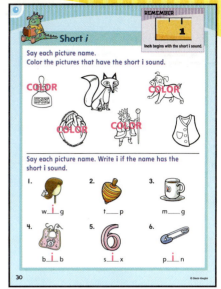

Short i

REMEMBER — Inch begins with the short i sound.

Say each picture name. Color the pictures that have the short i sound.

COLOR   COLOR   COLOR   COLOR

Say each picture name. Write i if the name has the short i sound.

1. w_i_g   2. t__p   3. m__g
4. b_i_b   5. s_i_x   6. p_i_n

Page 30

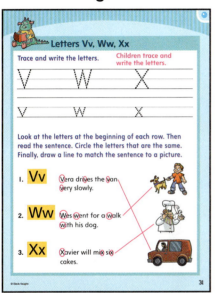

Letters Vv, Ww, Xx

Trace and write the letters.

Children trace and write the letters.

V W X

v w x

Look at the letters at the beginning of each row. Then read the sentence. Circle the letters that are the same. Finally, draw a line to match the sentence to a picture.

1. Vv — Vera drives the van very slowly.

2. Ww — Wes went for a walk with his dog.

3. Xx — Xavier will mix six cakes.

Page 31

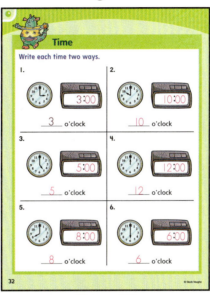

Time

Write each time two ways.

1. 3:00 — 3 o'clock   2. 10:00 — 10 o'clock
3. 5:00 — 5 o'clock   4. 12:00 — 12 o'clock
5. 8:00 — 8 o'clock   6. 6:00 — 6 o'clock

Page 32

Short o

REMEMBER — Ox begins with the short o sound.

Say each picture name. Color the pictures that have the short o sound.

COLOR   COLOR   COLOR   COLOR

Say each picture name. Write o if the name has the short o sound.

1. m_o_p   2. d_o_g   3. t_o_p
4. f__n   5. h__n   6. p_o_t

Page 33

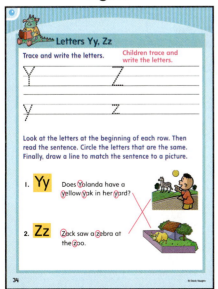

Letters Yy, Zz

Trace and write the letters.

Children trace and write the letters.

Y Z

y z

Look at the letters at the beginning of each row. Then read the sentence. Circle the letters that are the same. Finally, draw a line to match the sentence to a picture.

1. Yy — Does Yolanda have a yellow yak in her yard?

2. Zz — Zack saw a zebra at the zoo.

Page 34

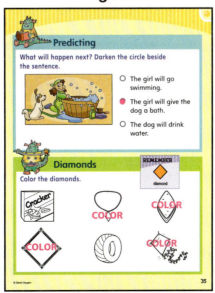

Predicting

What will happen next? Darken the circle beside the sentence.

○ The girl will go swimming.
● The girl will give the dog a bath.
○ The dog will drink water.

Diamonds

REMEMBER — diamond

Color the diamonds.

COLOR   COLOR   COLOR

Page 35

Numbers to 100

Write the missing numbers.

1	2	3	4	5	6	7	8	9	10
11	12	13	14	15	16	17	18	19	20
21	22	23	24	25	26	27	28	29	30
31	32	33	34	35	36	37	38	39	40
41	42	43	44	45	46	47	48	49	50
51	52	53	54	55	56	57	58	59	60
61	62	63	64	65	66	67	68	69	70
71	72	73	74	75	76	77	78	79	80
81	82	83	84	85	86	87	88	89	90
91	92	93	94	95	96	97	98	99	100

Page 36

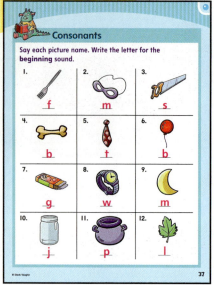
Page 37

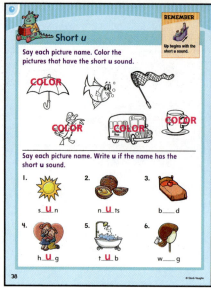
Page 38

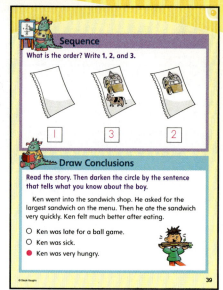
Page 39

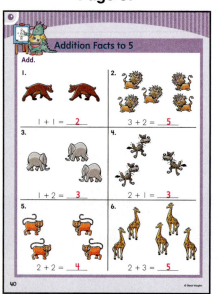
Page 40

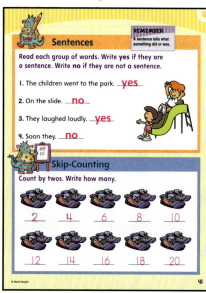
Page 41

Page 42

Page 43

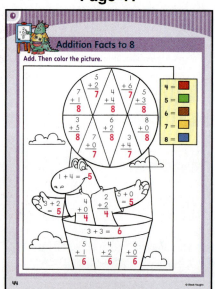
Page 44

Page 45

134

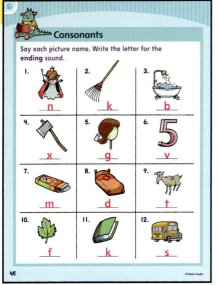

Page 46

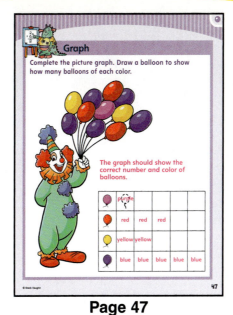

Page 47

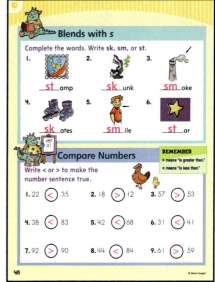

Page 48

Page 49

Page 50

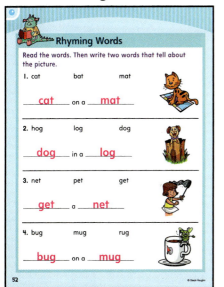

Page 51

Page 52

Page 53

Page 54

Page 55

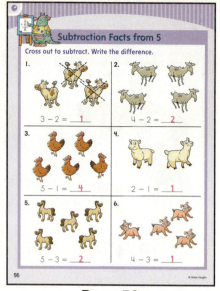

Page 56

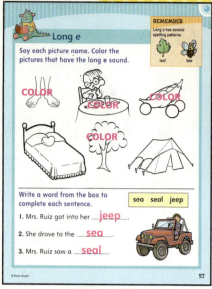

Page 57

Page 58

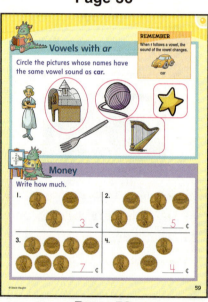

Page 59

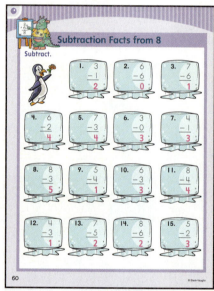

Page 60

Page 61

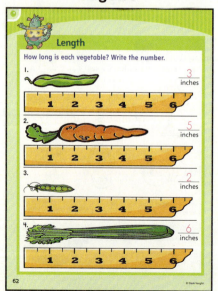

Page 62

Page 63

136

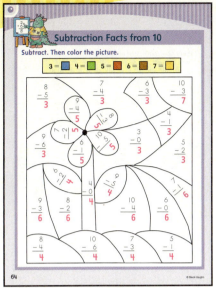

Page 64

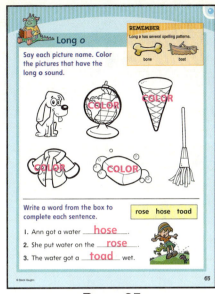

Page 65

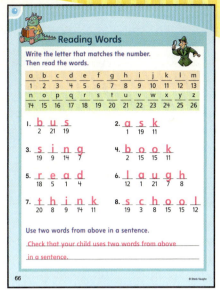

Page 66

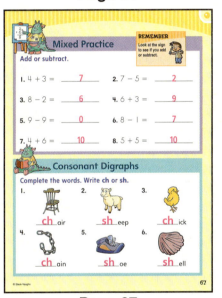

Page 67

Page 68

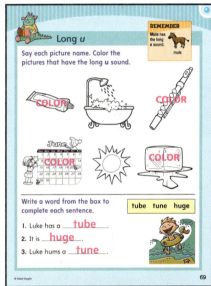

Page 69

Page 70

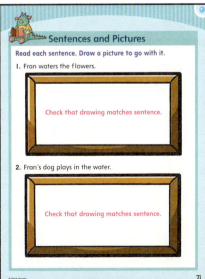

Page 71

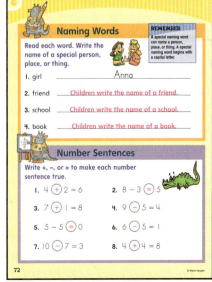

Page 72

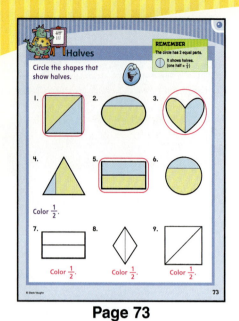

Page 73

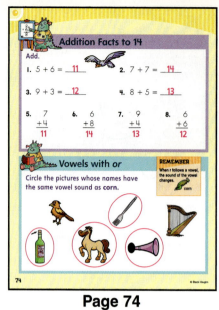

Page 74

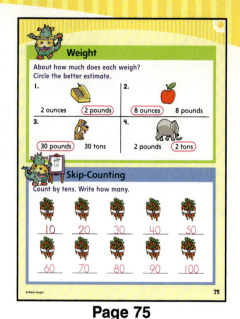

Page 75

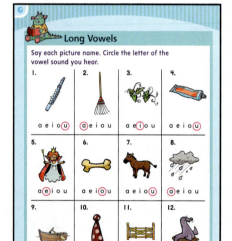

Page 76

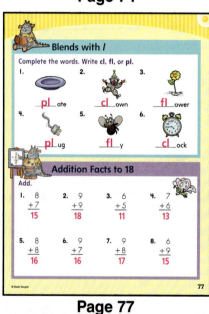

Page 77

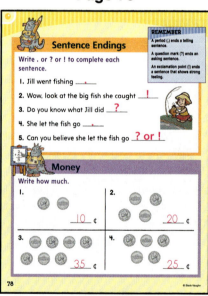

Page 78

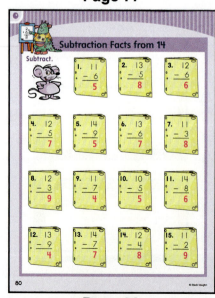

Page 79

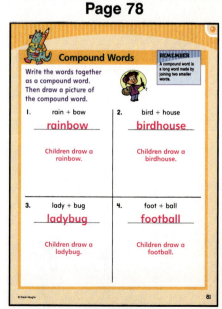

Page 80

Page 81

138

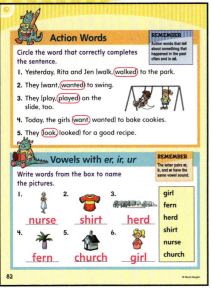

Action Words

REMEMBER: Action words that tell about something that happened in the past often end in ed.

Circle the word that correctly completes the sentence.

1. Yesterday, Rita and Jen (walk, **walked**) to the park.
2. They (want, **wanted**) to swing.
3. They (play, **played**) on the slide, too.
4. Today, the girls (**want**, wanted) to bake cookies.
5. They (**look**, looked) for a good recipe.

Vowels with er, ir, ur

REMEMBER: The letter pairs er, ir, and ur have the same vowel sound.

Write words from the box to name the pictures.

1. **nurse**
2. **shirt**
3. **herd**
4. **fern**
5. **church**
6. **girl**

Box: girl, fern, herd, shirt, nurse, church

Page 82

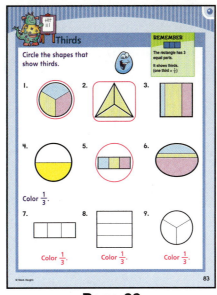

Thirds

REMEMBER: The rectangle has 3 equal parts. It shows thirds. (one third = $\frac{1}{3}$)

Circle the shapes that show thirds.

1. 2. 3. 4. 5. 6.

Color $\frac{1}{3}$.
7. 8. 9.

Color $\frac{1}{3}$. Color $\frac{1}{3}$. Color $\frac{1}{3}$.

Page 83

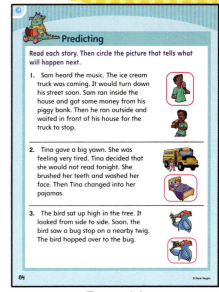

Predicting

Read each story. Then circle the picture that tells what will happen next.

1. Sam heard the music. The ice cream truck was coming. It would turn down his street soon. Sam ran inside the house and got some money from his piggy bank. Then he ran outside and waited in front of his house for the truck to stop.

2. Tina gave a big yawn. She was feeling very tired. Tina decided that she would not read tonight. She brushed her teeth and washed her face. Then Tina changed into her pajamas.

3. The bird sat up high in the tree. It looked from side to side. Soon, the bird saw a bug stop on a nearby twig. The bird hopped over to the bug.

Page 84

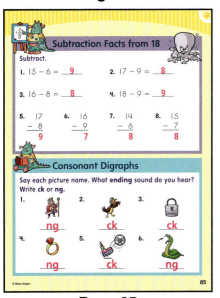

Subtraction Facts from 18

Subtract.

1. 15 − 6 = **9**
2. 17 − 9 = **8**
3. 16 − 8 = **8**
4. 18 − 9 = **9**

5. 17 − 8 = **9**
6. 16 − 9 = **7**
7. 14 − 6 = **8**
8. 15 − 7 = **8**

Consonant Digraphs

Say each picture name. What ending sound do you hear? Write ck or ng.

1. **ng**
2. **ck**
3. **ck**
4. **ng**
5. **ck**
6. **ng**

Page 85

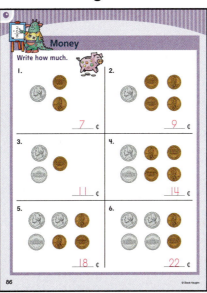

Money

Write how much.

1. 2. **7**¢ **9**¢
3. 4. **11**¢ **14**¢
5. 6. **18**¢ **22**¢

Page 86

Vowel Digraph ea

REMEMBER: The digraph ea can stand for two sounds. bread (short e), peach (long e)

Write the word that matches each picture.

1. **spread**
2. **pea**
3. **sweater**
4. **bead**
5. **thread**
6. **leaf**

Box: bead, pea, spread, thread, leaf, sweater

Main Idea

Read the story. What is this story mostly about? Darken the circle by the sentence.

Sam made a ball out of the snow. Then he rolled it around on the ground. Soon he had a big snowball. Sam made another snowball. But this one was smaller. He put it on the big ball. Then, Sam added two eyes, a nose, and a mouth. Sam thought his snowman looked great!

● Sam made a snowman.
○ Sam made a snowball.
○ Sam played with his friends.

Page 87

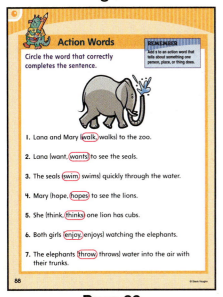

Action Words

REMEMBER: Add s to an action word that tells about something one person, place, or thing does.

Circle the word that correctly completes the sentence.

1. Lana and Mary (**walk**, walks) to the zoo.
2. Lana (want, **wants**) to see the seals.
3. The seals (**swim**, swims) quickly through the water.
4. Mary (hope, **hopes**) to see the lions.
5. She (think, **thinks**) one lion has cubs.
6. Both girls (**enjoy**, enjoys) watching the elephants.
7. The elephants (**throw**, throws) water into the air with their trunks.

Page 88

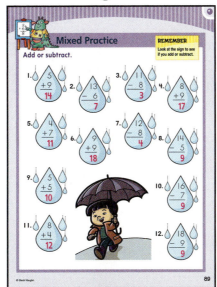

Mixed Practice

REMEMBER: Look at the sign to see if you add or subtract.

Add or subtract.

1. 5 + 9 = **14**
2. 13 − 6 = **7**
3. 11 − 8 = **3**
4. 8 + 9 = **17**
5. 4 + 7 = **11**
6. 9 + 9 = **18**
7. 12 − 8 = **4**
8. 14 − 5 = **9**
9. 5 + 5 = **10**
10. 16 − 7 = **9**
11. 8 + 4 = **12**
12. 18 − 9 = **9**

Page 89

Classify

Draw an X on the picture that does not belong.

1.
2.
3.
4.

Page 90

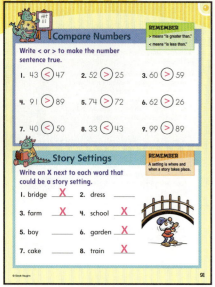

Compare Numbers

REMEMBER
> means "is greater than."
< means "is less than."

Write < or > to make the number sentence true.

1. 43 < 47   2. 52 > 25   3. 60 > 59
4. 91 > 89   5. 74 > 72   6. 62 > 26
7. 40 < 50   8. 33 < 43   9. 99 > 89

Story Settings

REMEMBER
A setting is where and when a story takes place.

Write an X next to each word that could be a story setting.

1. bridge X   2. dress ___
3. farm X   4. school X
5. boy ___   6. garden X
7. cake ___   8. train X

Page 91

Sentences

REMEMBER
Leave spaces between the words in a sentence.

Write each sentence correctly.

1. Afrogisgreen.

   A frog is green.

2. Frogsliketohop.

   Frogs like to hop.

3. Frogscanswim.

   Frogs can swim.

4. Theyeatflies.

   They eat flies.

Page 92

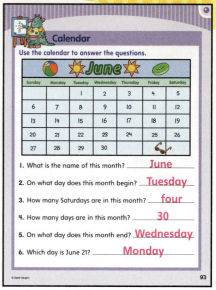

Calendar

Use the calendar to answer the questions.

June

Sunday	Monday	Tuesday	Wednesday	Thursday	Friday	Saturday
		1	2	3	4	5
6	7	8	9	10	11	12
13	14	15	16	17	18	19
20	21	22	23	24	25	26
27	28	29	30			

1. What is the name of this month? June
2. On what day does this month begin? Tuesday
3. How many Saturdays are in this month? four
4. How many days are in this month? 30
5. On what day does this month end? Wednesday
6. Which day is June 21? Monday

Page 93

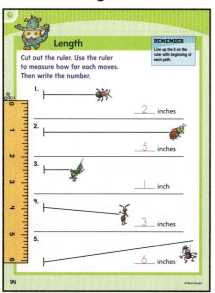

Length

REMEMBER
Line up the 0 on the ruler with beginning of each path.

Cut out the ruler. Use the ruler to measure how far each moves. Then write the number.

1. 2 inches
2. 5 inches
3. 1 inch
4. 3 inches
5. 6 inches

Page 94

Action Words

REMEMBER
When you add ing to a word that ends with a vowel and a consonant, double the final consonant.
chop   chopping

Add ing to each word.

1. trip   tripping
2. begin beginning
3. win   winning
4. run   running

Write a word from above to complete each sentence.

5. Lee and Tim are running a race.
6. The race is beginning now.
7. Tim is tripping over his shoelaces.
8. Lee is winning the race.

Page 95

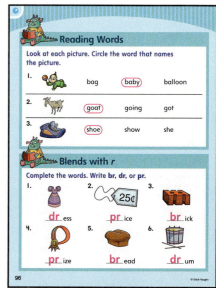

Reading Words

Look at each picture. Circle the word that names the picture.

1. bag   (baby)   balloon
2. (goat) going   got
3. (shoe) show   she

Blends with r

Complete the words. Write br, dr, or pr.

1. dr ess   2. pr ice   3. br ick
4. pr ize   5. br ead   6. dr um

Page 96

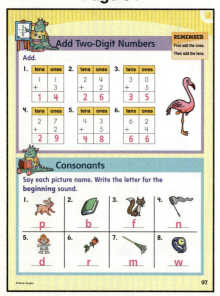

Add Two-Digit Numbers

REMEMBER
First add the ones. Then add the tens.

Add.

1. | tens | ones |
   |------|------|
   | 1 | 1 |
   | + 1 | 3 |
   | 1 | 4 |

2. | tens | ones |
   |------|------|
   | 2 | 4 |
   | + 4 | 2 |
   | 2 | 6 |

3. | tens | ones |
   |------|------|
   | 3 | 0 |
   | + 0 | 5 |
   | 3 | 5 |

4. | tens | ones |
   |------|------|
   | 2 | 7 |
   | + 7 | 2 |
   | 2 | 9 |

5. | tens | ones |
   |------|------|
   | 4 | 3 |
   | + 3 | 5 |
   | 3 | 8 |

6. | tens | ones |
   |------|------|
   | 4 | 2 |
   | + 2 | 4 |
   | 6 | 6 |

Consonants

Say each picture name. Write the letter for the beginning sound.

1. p   2. b   3. f   4. n
5. d   6. r   7. m   8. w

Page 97

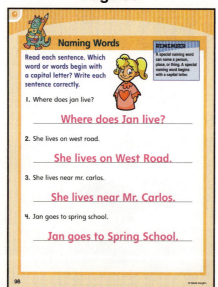

Naming Words

REMEMBER
A special naming word can name a person, place, or thing. A special naming word begins with a capital letter.

Read each sentence. Which word or words begin with a capital letter? Write each sentence correctly.

1. Where does jan live?

   Where does Jan live?

2. She lives on west road.

   She lives on West Road.

3. She lives near mr. carlos.

   She lives near Mr. Carlos.

4. Jan goes to spring school.

   Jan goes to Spring School.

Page 98

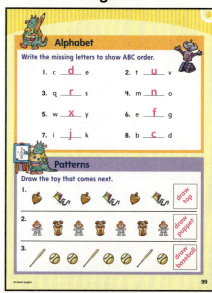

Alphabet

Write the missing letters to show ABC order.

1. c d e   2. t u v
3. q r s   4. m n o
5. w x y   6. e f g
7. i j k   8. b c d

Patterns

Draw the toy that comes next.

1. draw top
2. draw puppet
3. draw baseball

Page 99

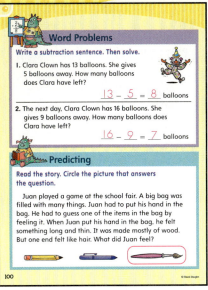

Page 100

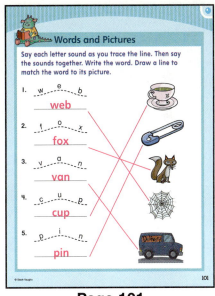

Page 101

Page 102

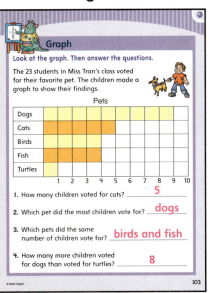

Page 103

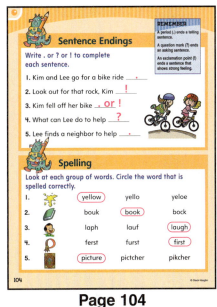

Page 104

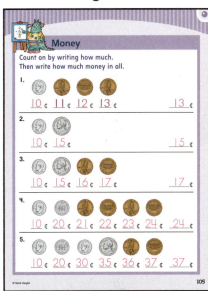

Page 105

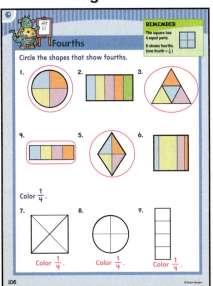

Page 106

Page 107

Page 108

141

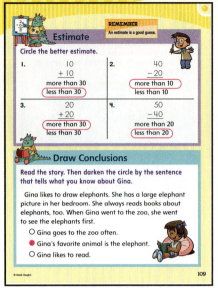

Page 109

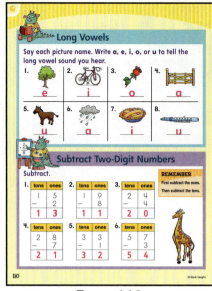

Page 110

Page 111

Page 112

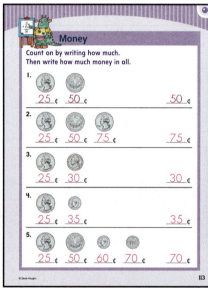

Page 113

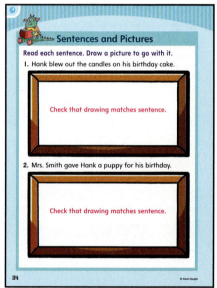

Page 114

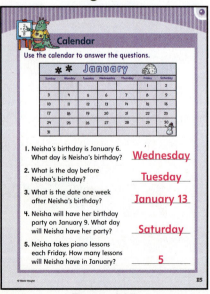

Page 115

Page 116

Page 117

142

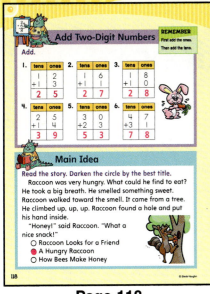

Page 118

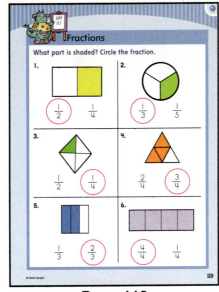

Page 119

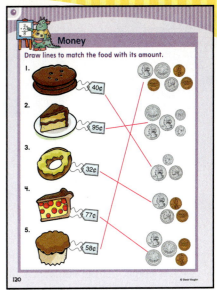

Page 120

Page 121

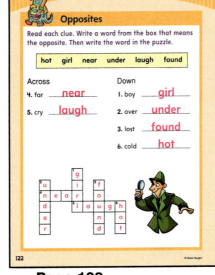

Page 122

Fun and Easy Outdoor Math Activities

Connecting Numerals and Quantities

- Take a nature walk with your child and gather different numbers of various objects, such as 1 pebble, 2 leaves, 3 twigs, and so on up to 10.
- At home, list the numbers 1 through 10 on a piece of heavy paper or cardboard. Next to the numeral 1, have your child place the single object. Next to the numeral 2, place 2 objects, and continue until all of the objects have been placed on the cardboard.

Skip-Counting

- Skip-counting is counting by 2s, 3s, 4s, 5s, and so on. Help your child select an object that can be skip-counted, for example, the number of wheels on cars, the number of wheels on bicycles, the number of legs on dogs, or the number of legs on birds.
- Take a walk and have your child begin counting the chosen object using an *adding on* strategy. When using *adding on* to count automobile wheels, he/she may say *one, two, three, four* at the first car, and at the second car, add on to four by saying *five, six, seven, eight,* and so on.
- Then together practice skip-counting (4, 8, 12, . . .) the same objects or different objects.
- After the walk, together make a chart like the sample below:

Number of Cars	Number of Wheels
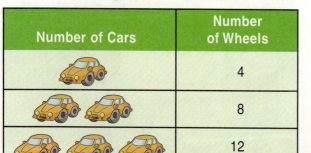	4
	8
	12

Shape Scavenger Hunt

- Go on a shape scavenger hunt with your child. Look for circles; ovals; triangles of all kinds; various 4-sided shapes such as rectangles, squares, parallelograms, trapezoids; pentagons (5 sides); and hexagons (6 sides) along the way.
- At home, have your child draw a scene including some of the things that you saw on your walk. Have your child describe the picture to you using the correct geometry names for the shapes.

Measuring End to End

- Find a place on a driveway, on a sidewalk, or a clear patch of earth. Mark a starting line with a stick in the dirt or with chalk on the pavement. Challenge your child to make a big jump. Mark the spot where he/she lands.
- Then ask your child to select a non-standard unit of measure such as a small, empty crayon box. To measure with such an object, your child will lay the box even with the starting line, mark where it ends, move the box to that mark, mark where it ends, and repeat this process until there is less than one box length left. You may want your child to estimate the fractional part of the box that is remaining. Together, count the spaces marked off to see how long a jump your child made.

NOTE

You may be surprised to know that these simple activities will help your child develop the important math concepts of number and operation, algebra, geometry, measurement, and data analysis and probability, as recommended by the National Council of Teachers of Mathematics!